Charlie Pye-Smith

World Conservation

Macdonald

ACKNOWLEDGMENTS

Many people have been kind enough to supply information for this book. Special thanks, however, must go to Richard North and to Epson UK Ltd, the former for letting me browse through his files and pick his brains, the latter for lending me a word processor which made the task of writing this book infinitely easier.

First published in 1984 by
Macdonald & Co. (Publishers) Ltd
London & Sydney

© Charlie Pye-Smith 1984

ISBN 0 356 10139 8

Macdonald & Co. (Publishers) Ltd
Maxwell House
74 Worship Street
London EC2A 2EN

A BPCC PLC company

Printed by Purnell & Sons (Book Production) Ltd
Paulton, near Bristol, Avon

BRITISH LIBRARY
CATALOGUING IN PUBLICATION DATA

Pye-Smith, Charlie
    World conservation. – (Debates series)
    1. Environmental protection – Juvenile literature
    I. Title II. Series
    333.7′2   TD170
    ISBN 0-356-10139-8

Contents

Conservation:

During his brief tenancy of the earth man has had a remarkable impact. He has been crafty, ingenious and inspired in his moulding of the natural world to suit his purposes. He has taken plants from the wild and through centuries of cultivation and selection developed much of the fodder which ends on our plates today. And he has taken a small number of wild animals and domesticated them, some as draught animals, others to provide milk and meat.

Man came out of nature and like the other creatures he has had to abide by her rules. However, so dramatic have been the technological advances and discoveries of the last few centuries that our relationship with the natural world has undergone profound and often dangerous changes.

The Indians on the American plains sought the bison with bow and arrow; but the white hunters introduced not only the rifle but the notion of mass slaughter: the bison was driven to virtual extinction. While modern firearms decimated populations of many animals, their habitats have been cleared to make way for settlements and farms.

This century has seen a revolution in farming techniques. The farmer – in the western world, at least – has at his disposal a huge armoury of pesticides and fertilizers. The former, in particular, have had severe effects on nature though their benefits in an increasingly hungry world have been many.

Why conserve? The disappearance of large numbers of species and their habitats may have serious consequences. Much that is happening today threatens 'the balance of nature'. The Amazon is thought to produce a third of the world's oxygen. Its destruction has implications for much more than that chunk of South America. The pollution of the air over industrial Britain affects more than its local climate and landscape – British acid rain is falling on Scandinavia and killing forests and fish stocks. The felling of forests in Africa for firewood removes more than the trees – it opens up the earth surface and enables tropical storms to strip the soil away.

According to Global 2000, a report commissioned by the former president of the United States, Jimmy Carter, 'hundreds of thousands of species – perhaps as many as 20% of all species on earth – will be irretrievably lost as their habitats vanish'. Not only shall we lose many creatures which are beautiful and attractive, but we shall be losing an immense stock of raw genetic material for which one day man's ingenuity may find a use.

Conservation and development Much of what happens today that sends animals and plants to extinction is the result of ignorance. And many observers of the world scene believe the poor are being forced to destroy the very resources on which their survival depends. Forests are felled not only out of stupidity or greed but necessity. Grasslands are overgrazed because there are just too many people trying to share them.

There will always be tension between economic development and the restraining necessity of conservation. And any book on the subject will throw up more questions than it can provide answers.

Is it inevitable that more great tracts of pristine forest come down and that the wild animals of the world are pushed into smaller and smaller areas? Does it matter if animals like the lion and the elephant are confined to small carefully policed national parks? And if the world's great wildernesses become populated and tamed to feed an ever increasing number of people, will we miss them?

Indeed, does it really matter if the blue whale, the Bengal tiger or the Arabian oryx – all subjects of this book – disappear from the face of the earth? After all, few now mourn the disappearance of the dodo. So why should those who live centuries hence regret the loss of species which become extinct today?

Opposite Since time immemorial the pastoralists of the White Nile swamps have shifted their cattle in synchrony with the seasonal ebb and flood of the river. The Jonglei Canal – one of Africa's biggest development projects – will affect both their traditional way of life and the ecology of the swamps (see page 30).

does it matter?

'Modern man talks of a battle with nature, forgetting that if he ever won the battle he would find himself on the losing side.'
E. F. Schumacher, economist

Too

'The era of the population explosion will necessarily be a short one.' *Erik Eckholm, ecologist*

many people?

Oh Calcutta! Many Third World cities can provide neither shelter nor clean water nor basic sewerage facilities for all their inhabitants. Yet their populations continue to swell.

One in ten of all the people that have ever lived is alive today. There are over 4.5 billion people in the world. By the end of the century there will be 6 billion. Hunger and destitution have become the lot of an increasing number. According to the United Nations Food and Agriculture Organization (FAO), 20 million people in 18 African countries faced famine in 1984. FAO estimates that everybody needs the food equivalent of 250 kilos of grain each year as a basic survival diet. 60% of the African population and huge numbers elsewhere in the Third World receive less than that.

So long as people are short of food both they and their environment will suffer. As increasing agricultural pressures overwork fragile soils, the ability of the environment to produce food diminishes. Though starvation is not exclusive to Africa, that continent provides us with the best example of the complex relationship between population growth, foreign aid policies and land degradation.

By the mid-'70s the eight countries with the highest population growth in the world were African. While the world's population grows at a rate of 1.7% a year (Britain, .007%; China, 1.2%; India, 2.2%), the African population grows at over 3% a year. At the present rate the population will double in 24 years. In order to feed itself at the end of the century Africa will need to double food production. Yet nine African countries are producing 10% less than they were in 1960 and per capita food production has fallen by a tenth since 1970.

Who's to blame? In 1793 Thomas Malthus published his famous Essay on Population. He said that while human populations may grow exponentially (for a while), food production cannot. Finite resources – of land, water, energy – mean that once the earth's carrying capacity is reached people must starve. Poverty, therefore, is inevitable; and Malthus blamed nature rather than human institutions.

This view has long been popular in the affluent West. Poor countries with high population growth can be conveniently blamed for their present plight: if African food production cannot keep pace with rising population then of course many must starve.

Others find such arguments both simplistic and objectionable. Were resources to be shared more equitably, they believe, the globe could support many more people than it does today: if all accessible land were actually to be cultivated by traditional methods we could feed between 8 and 10 billion people. They also maintain that there is evidence to show that populations that are educated tend to stabilize. It is only once basic health needs are assured that family planning programmes can have any chance of success.

Trade and aid policies of the West may also compound the problems of the poor. Aid programmes are often seen as too ambitious (with western-educated élites creaming off the main benefits), while countries relying heavily on cash crops are particularly vulnerable to fickle changes of policy in the consuming West.

'It is sheer hypocrisy to tell Africa to curb its population growth while thousands of African babies die daily from preventable diseases.' Grace Akello, journalist

Where is all our soil going?

In the West Indies scientists measure the fallout of topsoil in the atmosphere – topsoil that comes from Africa. Between 1970 and 1977 the fallout of topsoil from Gambia increased fourfold.

Soil erosion has become an enormous problem in the world's arid lands, which support over 600 million people. Even in America erosion is so bad that one third of cropland is threatened by decreasing productivity. In the last ten years 2 million hectares have been abandoned in Italy because of erosion and soil degradation caused by poor farming methods. The greatest erosion occurs on hillsides and in arid areas. Without the tiny crust of topsoil man cannot grow the crops to sustain himself or his animals.

The Sahel tragedy Between 1970 and 1973 some 200,000 people – mainly nomads and herders – died in the drought which struck the Sahel region of Africa. So did 3-4 million animals. The reasons for the tragedy were various. First, the rains didn't materialize. Second, since the 1930s the population has expanded rapidly and so have the numbers of livestock. In Niger the amount of land devoted to peanuts – a cash crop – increased from 73,000 ha in 1934 to 432,000 ha in 1968, thus putting more pressure on grazing lands. Nomads have been forced into settling and the richest lands have been overgrazed. Soil erosion has been the result.

The formidable Sahara Desert is expanding – west into Senegal, south into Niger and Chad, north into Algeria and Tunisia, east into Sudan. Since the drought, there has been a large Sahelian aid programme though, ironically, there have been instances of Tuareg and Bororo herdsmen in Niger asking the government to turn off water pumps and not build more wells as these have encouraged other tribes to move onto their pastures.

The future remains bleak: the population of the Sahel in 1975 was 25 million. It is expected to reach 40 million by the year 2000. More people means more animals which means ... Or does it? Should Niger grow less peanuts and more grain? Is it inevitable that the nomadic way of life must disappear when there is less and less space to go round?

A glimmer of hope The United Nations suggests that over the next 20 years $48 billion are needed to rehabilitate the land, but the money just isn't there.

However, a project in India's Shivalik Hills provides a good example of what can be done. Two centuries ago cattle ranchers moved from the plains into the hills as they ran out of land. They cut down trees and overgrazed the fragile hill soils. Annual crop yields fell dramatically. So serious was the plight of the hills that a reafforestation project was begun and cropping and grazing have been carefully regulated. Crop yields are now back to their former level.

The more fragile the soils, the more carefully must they be managed. It is a lesson that many countries are learning the hard way.

Opposite Contour ploughing on an Iowa farm. This is one technique commonly used to combat soil erosion on sloping farmland, both in the United States and elsewhere.

Below Bleached bones in Sudan's Kordofan province. This camel may have died from lack of forage, rather than lack of water. The desert in Sudan is said to have shifted 100 km south between 1958 and 1975. During the same period Kordofan's livestock numbers increased sixfold.

'Only a few inches of topsoil separate us from death.' *Edwin Peterson, ecologist*

Why bother with

Genes are the key to the future. They are an inheritance from past generations and a bequest to those which follow. It is through them that a plant or animal's successful traits can be handed on: resistance to disease and pests, the ability to survive drought or a capacity to produce heavy yields. Genes from wild plants are crucial for successful crop production on our farms. Had several wild tomato species with high disease resistance not been available we probably couldn't grow tomatoes commercially today. All modern cereals have been improved by wild genetic resources. A rare species of rice from central India doubled Indonesia's rice production.

> 'In a sense, we in the South are conserving our genetic resources for the North to exploit and enjoy.' Dr Emil Salim, Indonesian Minister of State

Seeds of hope? Most of our crops evolved in a small number of regions blessed with high genetic diversity. These regions and their genes are under threat. Loss of habitat, deforestation, overgrazing and pollution have all played their part in the extinction of genetic strains.

Further pressure comes from modern agricultural techniques, with their reliance on uniform strains. For example, hundreds of wild sugar beet strains are extinct in Turkey following the introduction of a single high-yield type. Ecologists are deeply concerned by the recent trend in seed patenting, with a small number of large companies dominating the business. Seed patenting enables companies to control agricultural practices.

Some firms are involved not only in seed distribution (and thus control of strains) but in the selling of fertilizers and machinery and in the marketing of the final product. In Europe bureaucratic 'streamlining' has led to a dramatic reduction in the number of vegetable and plant strains that can be marketed. During 1980 1,700 vegetable varieties were removed from sale in the European Community.

The United Nation's Food and Agriculture Organization (FAO) estimates that by 2000 two-thirds of all seeds planted in the Third World will be of uniform strains. This is potentially disastrous as only a varied genetic stock will help future farmers adapt to changing patterns of climate and disease.

Banking on a future The importance of gene reservoirs is now widely recognized and many Third World countries are realizing that genes are a valuable economic resource. The United Nations recently set up a committee to oversee the conservation and use of genetic resources. There are two ways in which the genes can be conserved: where they grow (India, for example, is planning sanctuaries to protect the wild relatives of banana, rice, sugar cane and mango), or in special gene banks.

Though little use has been made of wild animal genes, the time may well come when we also need them. It has been belatedly realized that we are losing an important breeding resource with the disappearance of old farm breeds. 115 of the 145 indigenous cattle breeds in Europe and the Mediterranean region are near extinction.

> 'Multinationals are patenting plant life and weeding out variety.' Mark Schapiro, ecologist

old genes?

Below There are about 2,500 North Ronaldsay Sheep on the Orkney island of that name. It is a small, hardy sheep which can survive on a diet of seaweed. The Rare Breeds Survival Trust is helping to save farmstock like this from extinction.

Right Rice paddies in Indonesia. High yields owe much to wild genes.

The disappearing

Almost half the world's species live in tropical moist forests, the richest and lushest habitat in the world. Only about one in six has been identified. Many will be extinct before we even know of their existence. There are five times more flowering plants in the forested Malaysian peninsula than in Britain, which is twice as large.

Despite their richness of vegetation, most tropical forests grow on poor, infertile soils. When cut down the soils often turn barren and useless. Consequently forest tribes have traditionally practised slash and burn agriculture. They fell an area, burn the trees, cultivate some crops, then move elsewhere so the soil never becomes exhausted. But with such practices a few people need a large area.

Getting the chop Since 1950 half the world's tropical forests have disappeared. In West Africa farmers clear 1,900 ha of dense forest every day. The Ivory Coast has less than a third of the forest which existed at the start of the century. In Amazonia a million trees are felled or burnt every hour. A quarter of all Central American forests have been destroyed since 1960 to make way for beef ranching.

Conservationists in the West argue that tropical forest destruction is one of the greatest contemporary tragedies. We could lose over a million species by the end of the century, most as a result of forest destruction. But can we blame the tropical forest countries – most of whom are poor, heavily in debt and have rapidly expanding populations – if they pull down their forests? Shouldn't they share the spoils of the earth? And shouldn't some of the blame for forest destruction be aimed at the affluent West? It is the West that demands the beef, and mahogany, a tree which will be commercially extinct by 1990. But if the tropical forests continue to come down at the present rate the real losers will be the people of Brazil, of Indonesia, of Madagascar…

Managing forests for posterity The great hope of turning tropical forests into rich farmland came to nothing. In the Amazon jungle there are now great swathes of bare, eroded land – memorials to unsustainable farming practices.

But forests can be managed in a way that provides a living for their dwellers, through agri-forestry. Rather than grow cereal crops or ranch cattle, the forest dwellers could cultivate a wide variety of trees, shrubs, cereals and other plants. The Lua hill farmers in Thailand, for example, cultivate 75 food plants, 21 medicinal plants and 31 other species. Such agri-forestry is best not only for the farmers but for the forest soils. The forests' survival will depend more on small-scale projects than on great 'get-rich-quick' schemes.

But most tropical forest countries will need help from the developed world to exploit their forests in this sustainable manner, and at the same time meet the demands of their growing populations.

'A tree is a tree. How many more do you need to look at?'
US President Ronald Reagan

forests

Forest clearance in Brazil's Amazon jungle.

The Amerindians:

The Save the Children Fund trains local health workers to help the Indians. Here one attends to a child with an eye infection.

adapt or perish?

Five centuries ago there were between 6 and 9 million Indians in Brazil. Today there are perhaps 200,000. The Amerindians' lifestyle is intimately tied to the rich habitat in which they live. They have a tremendous knowledge of the food crops and medicines of the forest – much greater than any of our scientists – and their culture has evolved over thousands of years to suit life beneath the trees. Yet the likelihood of many Amerindian tribes surviving is slight, except perhaps in reservations.

The reason for this is simple. Brazil is massively in debt. She sees her salvation in the exploitation of the forest resources. Apart from wood, Amazonia has deposits of oil, coal, iron ore and bauxite. The government has encouraged poor farmers to settle along the Trans-Amazonian highway, and low land prices have enticed agribusinesses and ranchers into the forest. Japanese and American companies have established giant pulp mills. In the rush to exploit the forest little account has been taken of the ecology of the region or of the needs of the indigenous people.

A tale of violence Death has been visited upon the Indians in many ways. A Brazilian government investigation in 1968 found that Cintas Largas Indians in the Mato Grosso had been bombed with dynamite. Most of the Beicos-de-Pan tribe succumbed after its food had been laced with arsenic. When opening up land for the Trans-Amazonian Highway in the early seventies, the army used bombs and machine guns against the Waimiri-Atroari group.

Between 1957 and 1963 tribes in the Mato Grosso were subjected to germ warfare. They were deliberately introduced to diseases such as tuberculosis and influenza, against which they had no immunity. The Nambiquara tribe numbered 10-15,000 in 1900. Disease, violence and the theft of its land by ranchers has reduced it to 530 individuals.

A future? Even if the remaining Indians are not subjected to such hostile treatment, it is unlikely they will survive long with their culture intact. The Brazilian government has pledged that it will designate land for the Indians to live undisturbed, but so far it has failed to carry out its promise. (Its apathy can be gauged by the fact that when the United Nations tried to draft a global action plan for tropical forests in 1982 Brazil did not take part.)

For some tribes the Xingu National Park has become a refuge, but the very designation of an area as a 'national park' points to the dilemma faced by those who wish to help the Indians, or the many other tribal peoples throughout the world whose existence is threatened by the destruction of their habitat.

Should the Indians be encouraged to adapt to 'modern' life? Or should they be left to continue their rich forest existence in splendid isolation? Indeed, what likelihood is there of them being left unmolested in countries like Brazil, where many of their poor compatriots are also fighting for their very own survival?

'One must prepare Indian people to live with the inevitable.'
Pia Maybury-Lewis of Cultural Survival

Fuel's paradise: a

Two billion people – about half the world's population – depend on firewood for fuel. In countries like Ethiopia, Sudan and Nepal nine out of ten people cook with wood or its derivative, charcoal. We hear much about the impending crises which oil shortages will bring; but little about the firewood crisis. It gets worse every year.

In central Tanzania between 250 and 300 days' work are needed to provide a year's firewood for a household. In some villages in Upper Volta, one of the countries in the African Sahel zone, women must spend 4.5 hours a day searching for wood. As firewood becomes scarcer the price rises. In one town in Upper Volta a cartload of firewood cost 350 francs in 1970, 1,000 francs in 1975, and 1,750 francs by 1979.

The firewood crisis further compounds the misery of the 700 million rural people described by the United Nations as the 'absolute poor'. In Sudan the demand for charcoal in the cities has led to armed skirmishes between commercial wood gatherers and forest rangers.

fertilizer. Indian farmers cannot afford to buy large quantities of artificial fertilizer; they must rely on animal dung to replenish the soil. But the firewood crisis is diverting dung from the fields to the stove.

Growing fuel In the early 1970s the oil producing nations of the world decided to use their 'oil power'. The dramatic price rises had a profound effect on the economies of western countries. Even worse hit were the poor countries. Their ability to develop has been severely restricted by the oil price rises and at the same time they have experienced increasing wood shortages. In the foreseeable future the only solution to the firewood crisis is for the countries which need it to grow it. Like any other crop, wood for fuel needs proper management.

Who should be responsible for establishing fuelwood forests – the local community, the country, or perhaps the World Bank? The women of Gambia who spend 360 days a year gathering firewood probably don't have time to think about it.

> 'We cut trees when they are too young...
> We must live on something. What else can
> we do?' *Sudanese wood-seller*

The ecological consequences The firewood crisis is an ecological Catch 22. Populations expand and more people require fuel. The poor can afford neither kerosene nor oil. They must have wood. The forests are felled too fast and turn to scrub. Scrub turns to desert. The gatherers must move further afield. And in many areas the exposed soils have been washed or blown away, so the chances of reforesting are slight.

In countries like India the scarcity of wood has forced rural communities to use more cattle dung as fuel. Today 10% of India's energy comes from dung – the equivalent of 60 to 80 million tonnes of organic matter and

thing of the past?

Right Decorated mud protects the heaps of cowdung from the monsoon rains. But can India afford to burn her dung?

Below Girls collecting firewood in Niger – a daily chore which gets harder day by day.

Collecting firewood has created a complete desert round Niamey, capital of Niger.

The tiger: back

The tiger is the Asian sub-continent's largest and most spectacular predator. Ten years ago it was on the verge of extinction. But 'Operation Tiger' – the largest and most successful conservation project ever established in Asia – has helped to swell its numbers. No-one knows how many tigers there were at the beginning of this century. There may have been around 40,000 in India. A census carried out in 1972 found a mere 1,827.

The reasons for the decline were many. Colonial hunters ruthlessly killed tigers for sport and trophies, and diminishing habitat led to a gradual decline. But after the last war the tiger population plummetted. More and more forest wilderness was brought under the axe and plough and the forests were exploited at an ever-increasing rate. Graziers poisoned tigers and poachers trapped them for their skins.

Since 1973, when the World Wildlife Fund helped set up Operation Tiger, the Indian government has acted with commendable skill and foresight, seeing the conservation of the tiger as a question of saving the entire ecosystem rather than just the species itself. The government introduced strict legislation to protect wildlife: tiger, leopard, elephant, gaur and several rare deer are included in a hunting ban. Poaching carries stiff sentences and is much reduced. Fifteen special tiger reserves have been established and the government and federal states spent over $10 million on the project during its first seven years. It has paid off. There are now over 3,000 tigers in India, about a third of them in the reserves.

What about the man-eaters? It is unfortunate for the tiger that one or two of their number adopt a catholic diet which includes human flesh. There are some villagers who bitterly resent the species' conservation. Between 1978 and 1982 four people were killed by tigers in the Chitwan National Park in Nepal. Between 3 and 5 people are killed or maimed by rhino every year in the same area. And since 1976 nearly 100 people have been killed by tigers in the Kheri District on the Indian-Nepalese border. Defenders of the tiger are quick to point out that thousands die of snake bites in India every year and hundreds are killed by elephants. (Though whether this is much of a defence is debatable.)

Operation Tiger has inevitably encountered opposition to its policy of shifting people out of the reserves and curtailing graziers' rights. About 6,000 people from 24 villages from Kanha National Park have been relocated. The operation, according to the WWF, has gone smoothly. Apart from the obvious benefits for the tiger, the project has also helped some of those who live on the reserves' edges: by providing direct employment, by attracting tourism and the service industries, and by conserving the soil and water resources of the forests.

But can the enforced migration of people from their ancestral homes be justified, to protect a species that they consider their natural enemy?

The Bengal tiger: beautifully camouflaged and deceptively serene, and saved on the brink of extinction.

> 'The tiger cannot be preserved in isolation. Its habitat, must first be made inviolate.' Mrs Indira Gandhi, Indian Prime Minister

from the brink?

> 'Certainly every tiger is a potential man-eater, in the same sense that every car driver is a potential man-killer.' Dr Paul Leyhausen

From reef to

Coral reefs – with their fantastic diversity of plants and animals – are the ocean's equivalent of tropical forests. Corals are half plant, half animal. The microscopic plants convert the sun's energy into food and dispose of the animal wastes. A myriad of other sea creatures live in the coral and at the apex of the intricate food chain are the fish, a vital resource for coastal communities. Architecturally and aesthetically coral reefs are among nature's finest achievements.

The threats The destruction of tropical forests is all too easy to see; the decline of coral reefs isn't. They are highly diverse ecosystems, yet any changes in the local environment can bring about the demise of an entire reef. Among the most damaging influences is pollution.

Were it not for reef-building coral, 400 islands in this world would not exist.

Though oil from ships has damaged some reefs, it is pollution off the land that poses the greatest threat. The stripping of forests or large engineering projects can result in soil erosion. The sediment is washed into the sea and reefs can easily be smothered. According to French expert Bernard Salvat, the introduction by European seamen of goats and sheep onto many tropical islands led to the destruction of natural vegetation and such heavy erosion that reefs suffered.

Reefs have also been destroyed by discharges of heated water from power stations, by sewage pollution and by the run-off of agricultural chemicals. The pesticide Lindane, for example, poisoned an entire coral reef in the Tokelau Islands of the South Pacific. Coral reefs have also been destroyed by more direct action: by the dredging of coral sand for construction purposes; by the use of explosives, both to extract coral itself, or as a drastic fishing technique; and by tourist developments and shell collecting (see page 22).

Saving the reefs The conservation of the world's reef systems is now seen as vital. The destruction of reefs can lead to the collapse of coastal fisheries and severe coastal erosion. Tropical countries can afford neither. Many also realize that the reefs are an important tourist attraction (and thus foreign currency earner).

One of the main ways in which protection has been sought is through the creation of marine national parks. However, conservationists argue that a network of national parks is not sufficient (in 1979 there were only 40 parks protecting coral reefs, many very small). If the world's coral reefs are to survive, then countries will have to control the sediment, sewage and agricultural pollution which enter their rivers, and also the types of fishing which can take place on and around the reefs. Again, say ecologists, it is a matter of exploiting the resource in a sustainable way: spears, nets and hooks are one thing; dynamite is quite another.

ruin?

'Fish are the first to desert the reef when environmental conditions start deteriorating.' *Bernard Salvat*

The crown-of-thorns starfish. For reasons never fully understood, it ravaged coral reefs off Australia and elsewhere in the 1960s and 1970s. Today the main threat to reefs comes from man.

The shell trade

Less than twenty years ago a visitor to Mombasa could swim out from the palms beside the ancient Kenyan port and float over magnificent coral reefs. Around the coral would swarm every imaginable type of fish; and over it would graze magnificent molluscs like the tiger, lynx and snake's-head cowries. These cowries, like many other shells, have had to pay for their beauty. The reefs off Mombasa have been virtually destroyed by coral and shell collectors.

As the reefs have been exhausted around Mombasa and the popular holiday resorts of Diani and Malandi, the shell collectors have moved further afield. By the mid-'70s the more remote reefs off Lamu Island in the north and Shimoni in the south were being stripped of their shells. Worse than the individual pickers – often women and children making little for their troubles – were the fishermen who dynamited reefs and skimmed whatever floated upward off the sea's surface.

But the men who really made money from the shell trade were the exporters selling large quantities to Europe.

A worldwide problem During the 1970s the world trade in shells escalated. The Philippines, Japan, Mexico and Haiti are the main suppliers of shells, and the main importers are the United States and Europe. By 1977 the United States was importing 4,600 tonnes of shells. Among the most popular species were the tiger cowrie, scallops, clams, nautilus (like an octopus in a shell) and cone shells.

Although much research remains to be done, the collecting of shells is known to have caused the decline of many species. The Australian Barrier Reef has been described as a 'graveyard for big clams': Japanese and

Taiwanese poachers are to blame. In the Caribbean and the Gulf of Mexico the queen conch and the flamingo tongue have declined as a result of collecting. And in Kenya the helmet shell (greatly favoured by Italian cameo-carvers) and the larger cowries have disappeared from heavily picked areas.

Nevertheless, molluscs have fantastic reproductive capacity and, although certain species have died out in certain areas, it is unlikely that any could become extinct solely as a result of collecting. The mining of coral for building material, oil pollution, and other factors which destroy habitat are probably the greatest threats to the survival of many shellfish.

Controlled harvests or bans? Some countries have taken measures to control the shell trade. Kenya introduced an export ban in 1979, the government controls shell collecting in Papua New Guinea, and in Australia certain species are protected. Some conservationists argue that there should be a total ban on collecting in many areas.

> 'Even reefs that are far away from everywhere have suffered from explosive fishing and from collectors.' Dr Rod Salm

But shouldn't local people be allowed to exploit a resource which can yield much-needed income? After all, many molluscs – mussels, clams, oysters, abalone – are harvested for food. Why shouldn't others be harvested for their beauty? And if anyone is to blame for the decline of species in tourist areas, shouldn't it be the tourists as much as those who collect the shells?

Right The tribes of East Africa have long used cowries as currency, as fertility symbols and as decoration. This Nyatura man in Tanzania, with his rows of cowries from ear to ear, is dressed for a dance.

Above Cowries, cones and conches – shells for sale in a Fiji market. Worldwide demand has led to a serious decline in the numbers of certain species.

Fishing: hooked

wo hundred years ago salmon was the staple diet for many estate workers in Scotland. Rather earlier Dr Johnson was feeding oysters to his cat. Both salmon and oysters are now delicacies, and overfishing fast threatens to turn other once common seafoods into luxuries. For centuries man has thought of the oceanic resources as limitless. In the 1960s the annual herring catch in the North Sea was around 900,000 tonnes. So severe was over-exploitation that by 1977 herring fishing had to be banned to allow stocks to pick up. The skate was common in the Irish Sea up to the 1940s. It is virtually extinct there now.

But the most spectacular recent example of overfishing comes from Peru, a country which developed the world's largest fishing industry in the 1960s. Until 1972 Peru led the world fish catch. The quarry was the anchovy. Scientists estimated that the maximum sustainable yield (the amount which could be safely taken year after year without stocks diminishing) was 9.5 million tonnes. Yet this was exceeded in 1967, 1968, 1970 and 1971. A combination of overfishing and a shift in ocean currents led to the collapse of the industry. The 1980 catch was under a million tonnes.

While herring declined in Europe, anchovy off Peru and haddock in the northwest Atlantic, African waters saw dramatic losses of hake, sardinella and pilchard. As the rich countries have overworked their own

> ## 'Ocean fishing today is oceanic anarchy.'
> *Jacques-Yves Cousteau, naturalist*

on growth?

stocks in northern waters, they have moved south to prey on the fish around the world's poorer countries. Inevitably, with their more sophisticated fleets, they have been better able to exploit fish resources.

Cause for concern? Opinions about the long-term implications of overfishing vary. It is obvious that the decline of certain species has been accompanied by the collapse of some fisheries: conservation of fish stocks makes good economic sense. On the other hand, some argue that provided fishing bans are imposed when species become seriously depleted they will always recover. Certainly, since the North Sea herring ban of 1977, the species has recovered in some areas. Often, of course, there are natural fluctuations: for example, the abundance of cod has risen markedly in the North Sea in recent decades. Natural fluctuations may thus obscure man-induced trends.

Who decides? The oceans, unlike the land, belong to no-one. It has taken the European Common Market over 10 years to agree a Common Fisheries Policy.

If friends have such difficulty in agreeing to controls and quotas on fish catches, what chance is there of countries traditionally hostile agreeing to oceanic fishing policies? Who should set the catch limits? Who should ensure that they are observed? And, most crucially, which countries should reap most from the marine harvest? Those with the technology best suited for exploitation? Those most in need of protein? Those who eat the most fish?

Far left An Indian woman and child gaze out to sea while a Peruvian anchovy fleet lies idle, victim of its own greed.

Left The spires of Inverness make a dramatic backdrop to this estuarine fishing scene. If the ancestral feeding grounds of the Atlantic salmon continue to be plundered in the north and west Atlantic, British salmon fishermen like these will lose their livelihoods.

Fish:

In 1975 92% of the Peruvian fish catch was turned into fishmeal, as was 79% of the Danish catch and 69% of the Norwegian. The beneficiaries of this industry were the pigs and poultry of the western world. Since 1977 industrial fishing fleets have taken half the catch in the North Sea: sandeels, Norway pout and sprat are all reduced to fishmeal. The catch of sandeels – a vital component in the marine food chain – has doubled since 1971. Unfortunately, industrial fishing operations often take many more species than those they are seeking. A considerable proportion of the whiting and haddock taken round Britain is a by-catch of industrial fisheries looking for Norway pout. And some of the species taken are vital for the survival of both other fish and many seabirds.

> 'The result of overfishing is that the annual world marine catch is 20% lower than it might have been.' *International Union for the Conservation of Nature*

A question of morality? In Southeast Asia fish provide 55% of animal protein, in Africa 19% and in North America 5%. The Japanese devour 30 kilos of fish per capita per year (compared to the British who average 7.5 kilos). They live on a small, densely populated island, and so rely heavily on marine rather than terrestrial protein. Carefully managed, the seas can provide the world with a large quantity of protein in perpetuity. It is the only large source of protein which

> A third of the world fish catch is diverted away from human mouths.

doesn't have to be cultivated or reared. Nature does all the work. It just remains for man to harvest sensibly.

Many people deplore the trend of using fish for feed rather than food. Those countries whose farmstock are fattened on fishmeal are the wealthiest and best-fed – indeed, overfed, according to many doctors. Thus, it is argued, it is wasteful, both in energy and in resource terms, to take fish from the sea to fatten stock. In a hungry world, every ounce of protein that comes from the sea should be used to feed people. Opponents of such a view will counter that market forces dictate present trends, that many of the species taken have no other use than feed (western consumers won't eat sandeels or capelin) and that marine protein would probably not be any more equitably shared than that grown or reared on land.

Overfishing may also have serious ecological consequences. The population crash of Norwegian puffins in the early 1980s was thought to be a result of whole areas being cleared of the seabirds' prey, the sandeel. There are fears that auk populations round Britain could suffer for similar reasons. Ecologists are also seriously concerned about plans to exploit the massive reserves of Antarctic krill (a tiny shrimpish creature). It has been suggested that the catch could rise from 50,000 tonnes (1977-78) to 60 million. Were the krill to be overfished the populations of other species would undoubtedly suffer. Five of the great whales (including the blue and humpback), three species of seals, and many seabirds and fish depend on krill. Certainly, say the ecologists, exploit the krill; but do so in a sustainable way. It remains to be seen whether the fishing nations have learnt from past lessons.

food or feed?

In a bay near Matare a whole Sri Lankan village goes fishing. Over 30 countries derive more than a third of their animal protein from fish.

Whales: a

Whaling is one of the world's oldest industries. There are now substitutes for every whale product used – for meat, oil, soap, candles, sperm oil, ambergris and whalebone. Yet whaling remains a merciless game of hide-and-seek with helicopters and massive factory fleets being used to find and process the whales. The big whales like the blue (which can weigh 150 tonnes) were hunted out first, and the whalers have shifted to smaller species as the larger quarry have dwindled. It is estimated that the population of the blue whale is just 3% of its original pre-hunting figure. For the humpback and bowhead, the figures are 4% and 5%.

The whaling nations have always argued that they have a right to continue whaling and that large numbers of jobs depend on the industry. The worst offenders in recent years have been Japan, the USSR and Norway. Unfortunately for the whales, their home is the last of the great global commons – the ocean: owned by no-one and subject to un-controlled and sometimes ruthless exploitation.

The protest Powerful protest movements have sprung up to save the whale. Groups like Greenpeace and Friends of the Earth have done much to heighten people's awareness

Greenpeace have shown remarkable courage in their efforts to foil the big whalers.

reprieve at last?

of the whales' plight. In 1946 the International Whaling Commission (IWC) was established to regulate whaling. It determines annual quotas and attempts to prohibit killing in certain areas. For years conservationists claimed the IWC was a whalers' whitewash, there to give respectability. And indeed during the IWC's life many species have been seriously depleted.

However, such has been the influence of the anti-whaling protest that there is now real hope that the whales will be left in peace. In 1982 the EEC banned the sale of all whale products except ambergris and whale tooth and bone ornaments. And in 1982 the IWC voted to ban all commercial whaling by 1985. Only three countries are opposed to the ban – Japan, Russia and Norway. Unfortunately, the IWC has no power to enforce its decisions.

Another dilemma Thousands of years before the advent of commercial whaling, aboriginal peoples in the Arctic relied on the whale for almost every conceivable need: oil for light and heating, meat for themselves and their dogs, bone for harpoons. The Alaskan Innuit traditionally hunt the now very rare bowhead whale. Over the last few years there have been heated rows at IWC meetings about whether or not these Eskimos should be allowed to take any of the whales. This is a dilemma which conservationists are likely to be confronted with more and more often as species traditionally hunted by aboriginal tribes are driven towards extinction. If it is ever a question of choosing between an Eskimo culture and the survival of the bowhead, which should we choose? And who should do the choosing?

Below A far cry from the industrial whaling fleets – a lone eskimo with a white whale which he has just harpooned.

'Norway has just been quietly getting away with murder.' Alan Thornton, Greenpeace

Wetlands:

'For the first time, local people will be able to trade livestock for grain. In drought years, being able to buy a sack of dura wheat is a matter of life and death.' *Anne Charnock, journalist*

This enormous machine (for scale, see man on left) chews its way through southern Sudan. The Jonglei Canal raises crucial questions about development planning and who should benefit.

down the drain?

The massive Sudd swamps, fed by the waters of the White Nile, are among the world's greatest wetlands, immensely rich in wildlife and home to pastoralists who for centuries have shifted their cattle to match the ebb and flow of the waters.

Egypt and Sudan, desperately needing more water for agricultural development, are jointly financing the building of the 350 km Jonglei Canal. When complete the canal will increase the downstream flow of the Nile by 5%, but reduce the water in the swamps. The canal is one of the most ambitious projects in Africa. It will not only provide more water but will improve communications, and thus trade, between the predominantly Arab north and the negro south, and the government hopes the region will also become an exporter of cattle.

Similar hopes lie behind the proposed development of the Okovanggo Delta in Botswana, another great wetland area. The government plans to wipe out the tsetse fly –

some other animals and birds, and there are fears that hunting along the canal bank will have serious effects.

Some believe Sudan would have been much better off with small, low budget projects – providing sources of clean water and basic health facilities, for example. So far Egypt and Sudan have spent $100 million excavating the first third of the canal.

Though the canal will bring benefits to the north, the way of life of the pastoral Dinka and Nuer tribes will be dramatically altered. The animist and Christian south deeply resents the political and economic domination by the Muslim north and many southerners see the Jonglei as yet another example of their resources being exploited for the benefit of others.

There are also serious worries about health risks. Schistosomiasis, a disease carried by water snail, is already a serious problem over much of Africa, particularly in irrigated areas. People who settle by the canal

'The canal will force a revolutionary change in the pace of life of the herdsmen.' The Economist *on Jonglei project*

which carries sleeping sickness – by spraying a pesticide over all the delta apart from the game reserves. The intention is to ranch cattle on all the tsetse-cleared area. Expansion of the beef industry will earn much-needed foreign currency.

But... the criticisms Both projects have their critics. The wildlife of the Sudd and the Okovanggo will inevitably be affected. The loss of habitat in the Sudd will lead to probable declines of the tiang, Nile letchwe and

will be at risk from the disease. In Botswana, there are fears about trying to ranch cattle in the Okovanggo. Wild animals provide a reservoir for trypanosomes, the parasites transmitted by tsetse, and are thus likely to cause infection of domestic stock.

Botswana has yet to decide whether to develop the Okovanggo. Meanwhile Sudan is contemplating further major canal schemes after the Jonglei. We shall have to wait some time to find whether it is the champions or the critics of the Jonglei who are proved right.

Ivory: Africa's

The African elephant is declining fast in some areas – though there are still well over a million left in the wild.

'Ivory has been steeped and dyed in blood.'

hard currency

vory, like gold and cattle, was an important currency long before the first banks. The Arabs who went slaving in the African interior sought ivory too. It often brought them greater wealth than their human quarry, who could be conveniently used as a means of transport. The main market, then as now, was the Far East. Japan and Hong Kong take four-fifths of Africa's ivory.

The resurgence of the world ivory trade in the 1970s led to exceptionally heavy poaching. Somalia is thought to have lost half her elephants in five years. Uganda lost 90% of hers during the decade, and poaching and drought led to the loss of half of Kenya's elephants between 1970 and 1977.

The ivory route With the Kenyan government's clampdown on illegal ivory trading in the mid-'70s, one of the main ivory routes became the Sudan, a country with about 130,000 elephants today. The ivory, much of which came from the Central African Republic and Zaire, was supplied with legally valid permits by Sudanese officials to circumvent the Convention on International Trade in Endangered Species (CITES).

Belgium only acceded to CITES in 1984. Since 1972, her airline, Sabena, has imported the rough equivalent of 40,000 elephants' worth of illegal ivory from Burundi. At least, the custom documents named Burundi as the country of origin of the ivory, but this is impossible as Burundi has no elephants!

Many poachers now use automatic weapons. The freedom fighter's friend, the Kaleshnikov AK-47, has become the elephant's enemy. And it seems that it is no longer just the mature bulls which are being selected for killing. The average weight of tusks imported into Hong Kong in 1978 was 9.65 kilos. For 1982 it was 5.39 kilos, suggesting that elephants of all ages are now being slaughtered.

Crop or poach? About half of traded ivory is poached; the rest comes from animals which have died naturally or been shot under li-

> **'Ivory and elephant products are part of a nation's wealth.'** Union for the Conservation of Nature

cence. Ivory is a natural resource that can be cropped, just as can be wild animals for meat. The real question is, who should share the spoils? Poaching tends to concentrate wealth in the hands of a few, whereas careful cropping programmes – which are often necessary to control elephant numbers where they conflict with agricultural man – could benefit the country as a whole.

The elephant certainly isn't as endangered as the African rhino and some scientists believe the scale of poaching is exaggerated. According to experts Ian Parker and Esmond Bradley Martin the numbers poached each year represent 'a very small proportion of the standing crop'. In the long term, the greatest threat to the elephant's survival will probably be the loss of its habitat as man takes more and more land for farming and settlement.

Caught in the act: poachers dismembering an African elephant.

The fur trade

Shortly after the European settlers invaded North America, the greatest wildlife slaughter ever known took place. Approximately 50 million bison roamed the wild west at the beginning of the last century. The Plains Indians depended on them for their survival. The bison provided both hides and meat. The slaughter began in 1826. The Indians were encouraged to join the carnage and according to expert Greta Nilsson, 'the near annihilation of the western bison came as a result of a deliberate campaign of the United States government to vanquish the Plains Indians by removing their means of subsistence'. By 1889 there were 541 bison left.

> 'If you've got it, flaunt it. I love my fur, on and off stage, and don't see anything wrong in that.'
>
> Bernie Winters, entertainer

Few hide- or fur-bearing species have suffered quite such a spectacular decline as the bison, but dozens have become dangerously rare as a result of hunting and trapping. A few, like the Falkland Island fox and the North American sea mink, have been hunted to extinction. As American populations of fur-bearing species plummetted, furriers began to look elsewhere. For example, between 1869 and 1891 the US imported each year over 100,000 skins of the East African Colobus monkey: consequently it is now very rare.

The big cats soon began to suffer too. Jacqueline Kennedy began a craze for cat coats after sporting a leopard in 1962. In 1968 the United States imported 9,556 leopard skins, 1,282 cheetah skins, 13,516 jaguar skins and 133,064 ocelot skins. Approximately the same number were imported by European countries. Wild populations couldn't carry such losses for long and many of the quarry species are now very rare.

'Vanity of vanities, all is vanity'? Conservation is often a matter of individual responsibility, and nowhere is this clearer than with the fur trade. The wearing of animal furs today has nothing to do with insulation – there are perfectly good woollen and (if you want to look like a tiger or a leopard) artificial substitutes: it is presumably a matter of vanity and status. The Convention on International Trade in Endangered Species (CITES) has done much to stem the slaughter of the cats and various seals, otters and other species. However, some important countries (for both importing and exporting) have yet to ratify CITES.

Widespread illegal trading also continues. For example, a container labelled 'mink' travelled from Ethiopia to Hong Kong in 1979, in which were found the skins of 319 cheetah, 31 leopard, 560 genet and 36 serval. The rarer the desired creatures become (and the stricter the legislation protecting them) the greater their monetary value. There are only about 1,000 giant panda left in the wild in China. In 1983 a dealer in Taiwan offered a panda pelt to an English journalist. The asking price: £17,000. If there are people prepared to pay this sort of money for an animal skin, is there much hope for creatures like the tiger, the cheetah and the snow leopard?

Endo dancers, some adorned with leopard skins and ostrich feathers, perform the snake dance at Tot in the Rift Valley. For them, the skins and feathers are part of their traditional culture.

This peregrine has been flown from India to West Germany with a live rock dove for its food. Highly prized for falconry, peregrines are taken from the wild in large numbers. This one is luckier than many: it has survived both capture and the journey.

Mynah birds should have kept their mouths shut. Had they done so pet fanciers and wildlife dealers might have ignored them. The mynah was once the commonest bird in Indonesian tropical forests. Collecting for the pet trade has made it exceedingly rare. For conservationists mynah birds have become a major worry.

The statistics Approximately 10 million birds are taken from the wild every year. Perhaps half die before they ever reach their destination. Two of the biggest traders are Senegal and India. Between 1970 and 1980 India exported nearly 15 million birds. The principal importing nations are the United States, Japan, Great Britain, West Germany, Belgium, Holland and France.

Before the last war the trade in cage birds was mostly confined to canaries and budgerigars. Over 70% of cage birds imported by the US in the first 40 years of this century were canaries. They now make up a mere tenth of the trade. Parrots, waxbills, lovebirds, weavers and many other exotic birds are now in heavy demand. And many are suffering serious declines. Approximately one million parrots are bought each year. Many more are mutilated or die of stress.

The bird trade is both wasteful and cruel. Methods of capture – which include netting, liming, trapping and wing-shooting – maim and kill many. A study by Jean-Yves Domalain found that 40% of the birds captured in Senegal died at the time of capture or soon after. In one of the worst cases, 2,029 out of 2,120 birds (parrots, waxbills and starlings) died on their way to England on an Air India flight. The airline was fined £2,400, but it later appealed successfully against the conviction.

There is also much illegal trafficking of birds which are supposedly protected by the Convention on Trade in Endangered Species (CITES). There is big money in the bird trade. Some of the rarest parrots fetch over £3,000 each. And as the birds become rarer those who seek them are prepared to pay higher prices. Perhaps it is not surprising that there are less than 30 magnificent Puerto Rican parrots left in the wild.

Clamping down As long as people in rich countries are prepared to pay for the fauna of the poorer nations and governments allow such trade to continue, many of the world's most beautiful birds will continue to decline. Conservationists believe that trade in birds should be restricted to those which have been reared in captivity. Were such a measure introduced there would be a dramatic decline in wild bird trapping.

But conservation is also a matter of personal responsibility. Those who buy cage birds should realize that for the one which makes it into their living room many die on limed twigs, in overcrowded cages and in aeroplanes and pet shops. So long as they patronize the trade they must share culpability for the loss of birds from the wild.

The fowl trade

'Taking their place with Gucci bags, Mercedes 450 SLs and Perrier, exotic birds are the hottest thing in pets from L.A. to New York.' *Greta Nilsson*

Bats: just

N̲o other sector of the animal kingdom has received such a bad press as the bat family. The Old Testament described the bat as 'an abominable thing' and exhorted man not to eat it. He seldom does; but this doesn't stop him from killing bats. The bat has been commonly associated with evil, and prejudice against bats is still rife. Odd ones like the South American blood-sucking vampire have done little to enhance the group's reputation. However, most bats are harmless and the insect-eating ones, which are the majority, are positively beneficial. They are nature's insecticide – absolutely safe and free.

'Even those species that seek sanctuary in churches cannot expect much Christian charity.' B. W. Yalden & P. A. Morris, ecologists

Throughout the world a wide range of bats are threatened. For example, in Britain, where all 13 species are protected by law, the mouse-eared bat is on the point of extinction (there are two males and no females left) and virtually every other species has declined in recent years. The greater horseshoe bat, which numbered tens of thousands not long ago, is now down to about 2,000.

The bats epitomise the problems of conserving species which are subject to a range of threats. And unfortunately their lifestyle just conspires to make things worse. They breed slowly and populations cannot make rapid recoveries.

The threats Farming practices have changed much since the last war. Pesticides

hanging on?

All British bats are now protected by law. These greater horseshoes are among the rarest.

and insecticides are routinely used and the numbers of insects in the countryside have declined. Thus there is often not enough food available for the bats. (Even the tiny pipestrelle can eat over 3,000 insects in a night.)

Farmers have also been ripping out hedges and chopping down trees, many of which were roosting sites for bats. At the same time local authorities and landowners have been closing up or filling in the caves and mine shafts which are often important winter hibernating sites for bats. Many colonies have been evicted by householders who dislike the idea of having bats in their roofs, and some vicars have taken similar action in their belfries. Chemical treatment of timber for woodworm has also contributed to the decline. As if all this wasn't enough, the popularity of pot-holing has led to bats being disturbed during hibernation. So sensitive are the creatures during their winter sleep that even slight disturbance can lead to death.

The law to the rescue Over the past decade bats have received much publicity – and a better press. Some landowners have erected bat boxes (like upside-down bird boxes) and an increasing number of interested people have helped naturalists' trusts to monitor colonies.

The bat, with its natural disadvantage of being a remarkably ugly creature, also has the misfortune of being nocturnal. When birds like the eagle or the corncrake decline we notice their absence. Bats, however, are rarely seen, but that does not lessen their value to us.

The pesticide dilemma

In the early 1950s there were about 75 million cases of malaria in India. By 1961 there were just 49,000. The World Health Organization's eradication policy was triumphing over the *Anopheles* mosquito, the beast responsible for transmitting the debilitating and often fatal disease. The weapon was the persistent pesticide DDT. In 1970 WHO estimated that the programme had prevented 2,000 million cases of malaria and saved 15 million lives worldwide.

But hopes of outright success in this pest war have been rudely shattered. By 1976 Indian malarial incidence was back to 6.5 million cases. By 1978 over 50 species of *Anopheles* mosquito had developed resistance to at least one insecticide. The mosquitoes were just some of the many disease-transmitting, crop-chewing creatures staging a fight back against the human chemical armoury. In 1954, 25 insects, mites and ticks were resistant to pesticides (those carrying the resistant genes surviving and handing resistance to future generations). This figure is now over 400.

A high price to pay? If man is to feed himself and combat many diseases he must control the organisms which vie with him for his crops and those which transmit such diseases as yellow fever, malaria and typhus. But in many cases over-reliance on chemical warfare is proving disastrous. Apart from escalating resistance problems (700,000 acres of cotton-producing land were abandoned in Mexico in 1970 because the tobacco budworm had developed pesticide resistance), many pesticides – particularly the persistent organo-chlorines like DDT – have devastated wildlife. Few pesticides kill just the target species. Most kill beneficial insects and other creatures which can help to keep pest populations in check.

The pest war: de-escalation In an ideal world, pests would be controlled by a whole range of techniques. Many ecologists believe the future lies in integrated pest management (IPM) where farmers are encouraged to combine moderate use of pesticides with age-old techniques such as crop rotation (which prevents the build-up of pests and diseases) and modern methods of biological control.

The latter involves pitting one animal or plant against another. For example, in the 1930s the Australian state of Queensland suffered a plague of prickly pear. The caterpillars of an Argentine moth (*Cactoblastis*) were introduced and they took just five years to munch their way through the infested 20 million hectares.

At the same time, aid organizations are stressing the need to restrict the sales of dangerous pesticides – often banned in the countries of origin – to third world countries. Apart from the devastation of wildlife, the toll of human casualties is ever-increasing. In 1972 WHO estimated that over 9,000 deaths a year were caused by pesticide poisoning. But despite all the problems created by pesticides, the overall success of the malaria campaign forces us to ask ourselves: isn't it worth it if so many lives are saved?

Opposite A spray team – armed with simple pumps and buckets – tramps its way to an isolated village in India. These teams are in the front line in the war against malaria.

> 'If there had been a world ban on DDT then Rachel Carson's book "Silent Spring" would be killing more people in a year than Hitler killed in his whole holocaust.'
> Dr D. G. Hessayon, Chairman of British Agrochemicals Association

'Speak now or forever hold your breath.'
Banner hung from chimney of Southern Electric Company, Ohio, by two climbers (both fined $250 and imprisoned for three days)

Time to stop dropping acid?

I n Norway fish have died out in over 13,000 square km of lakes. In Germany's Baden-Wurttemberg region – which includes the famous Black Forest – half of the trees have been damaged; the same has happened in Bavaria. The culprit is acid rain. It threatens to give us one of the worst environmental headaches imaginable over the next decade. Agricultural productivity may be impaired and magnificent buildings like the Taj Mahal and the Acropolis are already suffering severe damage.

Acid rain is formed when sulphur dioxide and various nitrogen oxides combine with rain water. Pure rain water has a pH (the standard measure of acidity) of 5.7. Rain over much of Western Europe and the industrial American states has a much lower pH (and thus higher acidity), sometimes dropping as low as pH3. The increase in acidity in fresh waters leads to impaired reproduction in fish, with salmon, trout and roach being particularly susceptible. Once the pH falls below 5.5 small species of mollusc and crustacean disappear and no fish survive once it falls below 4.5 (in 15 states east of the Mississippi the rain has pH values between 4.8 and 4.1.)

Whose problem? The main sources of the emissions which turn to acid rain are electric power stations and oil refineries. Britain is Europe's biggest emitter of sulphur dioxide (producing over 4 million tonnes in 1982). Over half is said to come from electric power stations. But of this huge quantity only a third falls on Britain. The rest goes elsewhere, ignoring state boundaries and the niceties of international law. Three-quarters of the acid rain which falls on Norway and Sweden comes from other countries. Half of Canada's drifts over from the United States.

Some scientists and industrial leaders say the scale of the problem has been exaggerated. It is undoubtedly difficult to separate the effects of acid rain from those of other aerial pollutants, and so far, claim some scientists, evidence which links acid rain to decreased forest productivity is circumstantial.

Big industry: time to come clean? Every year between 30,000 and 90,000 tonnes of lime (a neutralizing compound) is spread on Swedish lakes to counter the effects of acid rain. But this is no long-term solution. The only long-term, viable and permanent cure is for the industries responsible for acid rain to reduce their emissions. Power stations could use fuels with lower sulphur contents and gases which are being released into the atmosphere can be 'scrubbed' to remove the sulphur dioxide.

But this is an expensive process. The Central Electricity Generating Board in Britain has threatened to increase electricity prices by some 15% if it is forced to reduce sulphur dioxide emissions. Some environmentalists say this is a scare tactic. But if it isn't, will the British consumer be prepared to pay to save the Swedish salmon?

Opposite Smoke billows out from a coal by-products plant at Cwm Colliery in Wales. Much of Britain's aerial pollution is carried across the North Sea to fall as acid rain on the European mainland.

> *'Acid rain is responsible for damage to nature on a vast scale.'*
> European Parliament's Environment Committee

Left Embalmed in oil, a stricken guillemot.

Below Oil gushes from the floundering Amoco Cadiz. The tanker's steering failed and she became stranded on the French coast near Brest, causing massive pollution.

Black gold: a high price to pay?

On a spring day in 1967 the Torrey Canyon oil tanker hit a reef 25 km west of Land's End. Within a few hours 30,000 tonnes of crude oil poured into the sea. A storm broke the back of the ship and more followed. Oil spread across Cornish beaches and some reached the French coast. The Torrey Canyon disaster was Europe's first big oil tragedy. 25,000 birds were killed by the oil.

Oil pollution affects the seas worldwide. One of the areas worst hit has been the sea around Europe. There have been been good years and bad years. In 1978, for example, there were 50 oil spills around Britain alone. The 14 largest killed over 10,000 birds. In 1981, 60,000 birds died in two Baltic spills. Although it is the big spills and oil-well blow-outs which hit the headlines, much of the oil pollution is caused by illegal discharging from boats and by pollution of our rivers, particularly with engine oil from motor cars.

The victims The massive seabird colonies around her coast are Britain's greatest claim to fame in the natural world. Every summer over a million pairs of guillemot, puffin and razorbill nest on British cliffs along with three-quarters of the world's gannet population. They are joined by gulls, shearwaters, terns, cormorants and petrels. Guillemots, razorbills and puffins have been particularly hard hit by oil pollution. 60% of the Baltic victims were guillemots.

When the Esso Bernica hit a jetty at Sullom Voe terminal in the Shetlands in 1978, the escaped oil polluted 65 miles of beach. Within eight weeks over 3,500 bird corpses were recovered. They included over a quarter of the islands' black guillemot population and 147 great northern divers, only 300 odd pairs of which breed in Britain. Otters and sheep were also among the casualties.

British estuaries are also world famous for the huge populations of geese and wading birds which descend on them during the winter months. With the dramatic increase in oil traffic over the last decade they have come under increasing threat. In 1983 an Iranian tanker collided with a jetty in the Humber and 6,000 tonnes of oil escaped. Conservationists predicted an environmental disaster. There were 20,000 wildfowl and waders in the estuary at the time. Fortunately losses were much lower than anticipated. However, had the accident occured two months earlier when there were 70,000 birds in the Humber, the toll could have been very high.

Keeping oil off troubled waters Conservationists believe much too little money is being spent by governments and oil companies on curbing pollution at sea. They also claim that marine surveillance and law enforcement are too lax. When offending ships' captains are prosecuted the fines are often derisory. And, of course, one of the problems is determining who should have responsibility for exercising controls in mid-sea. The European Commission has been critical of both oil companies and governments, which it claims have failed to learn all the lessons of past spills.

There is little the individual can do to stop the spills at sea. What we can do, however, is to ensure that the oil we empty from our cars doesn't end up floating down to sea.

Wilderness:

The Australian state of Tasmania has high unemployment. It also has one of the world's great wilderness areas – 13,000 square km of temperate rainforest. The forest is uninhabited, uncultivated and, for the most part, unexplored.

Such is the quality of the wilderness that UNESCO has classified it as a World Heritage Site, along with other such jewels as Katmandu Valley, the Grand Canyon and the Pyramids. The Franklin River, which runs through the wilderness, is the only major Tasmanian river which has not been dammed. The wilderness contains endangered species like the Tasmanian devil, marsupial mouse, spiny ant-eater, duck-billed platypus and orange-bellied parrot. The forests contain a third of the world's Huon pine, a tree which lives to be over 2,000 years old, and many valuable archaeological sites.

It was just the sort of propaganda coup needed by the conservationists. Work at the dam was halted and Australia's newly elected prime minister declared that the dam would not be built.

Room for wilderness? A wilderness can be defined as a large area where the hand of man is absent. The greatest is the continent of Antarctica. Others are found throughout the world. Invariably, wildernesses support animal and plant communities of great value. But their real importance lies not just in the biological worlds they encompass but in their very remoteness and emptiness.

Many of the people who have argued most passionately for wilderness preservation have explained their concern in spiritual terms: man has a need for vast spaces where few venture. Just as Mecca is as important to

A colony of king penguins in the wilderness of Antarctica.

> '*US Interior Secretary James Watt is not selling off Federal wilderness lands to private developers just because there's money in it. No, Secretary Watt is doing it because Jesus tells him to.*' David Helton, journalist

But the Tasmanian state government decided that jobs were more important than wilderness. It put its backing behind a hydroelectric power scheme whose dams, if built, would flood over 16% of the wilderness. The scheme was to create 1,000 jobs over the ten-year construction period.

The plans caused international furore. The Tasmanian Wilderness Society campaigned vigorously to stop the project and conservation groups round the world added their support. Celebrated botanist David Bellamy flew to Tasmania, helped blockade machines which had already begun to rip down forest, and spent his fiftieth birthday in jail.

a Muslim who never makes the pilgrimage as to one who does, so the idea of wilderness is said to inspire many who can never actually experience it.

To others, such ideas are just so much hot air. People, they say, are more important than empty spaces. The Antarctic has huge resources – both animal and mineral: we should exploit them. And if the development of a wilderness area will bring jobs and prosperity, then surely we should develop it.

As the world's population fast increases, does it mean that wildernesses will soon become a luxury we can ill-afford? Or does man's spiritual welfare depend on their survival?

an empty luxury?

'Let man go into the wild places and his indifference is shattered.'
Sir Laurens van der Post, writer

Parks

'National parks cannot survive when surrounded by a hostile population waiting for any opportunity to move in and exterminate the wildlife.' Dr Walter Lusugi, ecologist

or peasants?

How the minibus got its spots – a leopard ponders the strange and garish world of tourism.

The best way to protect the world's wildlife is by protecting large areas of land – in national parks or nature reserves. Just over 1% of the earth's land surface is so protected (about half of which is in North America) but ecologists say this is nowhere near enough.

Moreover, in many third world countries population growth, land hunger, poaching and lax law enforcement often conspire to degrade areas which are supposedly protected. For example, in East Kalimantan in Sumatra a third of a 20,000 ha reserve has been appropriated for logging. And in Kenya, 2,750 ha were recently excised from Nakuru National Park to resettle 6,000 families; thus over a third of the park was lost. There have been reports that 10,000 ha have been taken from Volcanoes Park in Rwanda to grow pyrethrum and another 4,000 ha for grazing domestic stock. In Brazil, a quarter of the Xingu National Park has been lost as a result of highway construction.

But people have suffered too. Many countries in the third world had a network of parks imposed upon them by colonial rulers. In Kenya native Africans have since time immemorial lived among the wild game and exploited it in a sustainable way. There was no major conflict between man and nature before the arrival of the European.

But under colonial influence the wildlife suffered considerably and after the Second World War a system of national parks was established. People were uprooted from their homes and resettled elsewhere – often on poor land – and all forms of subsistence hunting were banned. Consequently the sup-

posed conservation of wildlife has led to much bitterness among the native people dispossessed because of it.

Most Africans find the tolls on park entry beyond their means and the laws which insist entry must be in cars prevent the majority from visiting the parks. Critics of the park system admit that wildlife-based tourism is important (in Kenya tourism is the biggest earner of foreign currency) but they resent the fact that large areas are now frequented mainly by affluent visitors from the developed world.

An inevitable conflict? 'Why should we conserve the last remaining five Java tigers at the expense of relocating the population away from its habitat area?' asked the Indonesian minister, Emil Salim. Such dilemmas threaten to become ever more common in the future. On one hand, more and more land is required to sustain growing populations. On the other, more and more land must be set aside and given legislative protection if the earth's wildlife resources are to be protected.

But must man and nature always live apart? Is it a straight choice between parks and peasants? The problem with many national parks – such as those in Kenya – is that they were established without consideration of the needs of local people. There is no reason why people must always be excluded from such areas; there is no reason why man shouldn't exploit both animal and plant resources within such areas, providing exploitation is carefully controlled.

Nature's

In Namibia's Etosha National Park scientists are putting lions on the pill. An 800-km fence round the park has prevented the seasonal migrations of wildebeest and other hoofed creatures, and boreholes created to provide water throughout the year have attracted the lions' prey so successfully that hunting has become a simple task. While wildebeest populations fell from 25,000 in the mid-1950s to 2,500 today, the lion population shot up. Normally 3 out of 4 cubs die in their first year. In Etosha life is so easy that most survive.

The Erie Canal in the USA was opened in 1825. It links the Great Lakes to the Atlantic. The sea lamprey, a creature which attaches itself to fish, sucks blood and often causes their death, came along the canal and gradually invaded the lakes. During the 1930s the annual catch of trout in Lakes Huron, Michigan and Superior was 6,400 tonnes. In 1960 it was 230 tonnes. The newcomer, with a little help from overfishing and pollution, had upset the balance of nature.

Some ecosystems tend to be stable – particularly the most diverse ones in tropical environments. Others experience great fluctuations – a crash in the population of one species may be followed by a corresponding drop in the numbers of one of its predators. But the delicate balance of the natural ecosystem can easily be upset by man.

In the early days of seafaring the introduction of goats, pigs and rats on tropical islands caused drastic vegetation changes and the

balancing act

In the Highlands of Scotland red deer graze without fear of natural predators. The wolf has long since gone. So high is the deer population in some areas that the native pine forest is being heavily overgrazed and is no longer regenerating.

decline of native fauna. The dodo can blame European sailors, rats and dogs for its demise.

In some instances man's deliberate extermination of predators has led to the explosive rise in populations of the prey species, turning once benign creatures into economic pests. Such has become the American white-tailed deer. The population is now 13 million and the deer is a major nuisance to farmers. Bobcat and coyote – both persecuted by man – are now too scarce to control the deer population.

Striking the right balance Many of the disasters which befall nature result from human ignorance: alien species are introduced without thought of the possible consequences; others are cropped too heavily; major en-

gineering or irrigation works disrupt migratory patterns. There can be no general rules about 'maintaining the balance' and indeed the mechanisms which control and limit animal populations are still not fully understood by ecologists.

Some countries, particularly the US, insist on Environmental Impact Assessments (EIAs) being carried out before major developments are undertaken. Scientists can then try to predict what changes a development may cause and action can be taken to minimize ill-effects. Inevitably, relationships between pest and prey are often so severely unbalanced that positive management techniques are needed. It may mean putting predators on the pill or regularly culling species whose natural predators are no longer doing their job properly.

A last resort?

Oman lost its last wild Arabian oryx, the nearest thing outside the Bible to a unicorn, in 1972. It was probably the last wild oryx anywhere on the Arabian peninsula. Fortunately for the oryx its demise had been foreseen and in 1962 a group of conservationists captured a small number of the few that remained and began a 'captive breeding' programme. A world herd was established at Phoenix Zoo in Arizona and the oryx bred so successfully that herds have been set up in other zoos in the US, in Europe and in the Middle East.

> 'Even the most wildly successful captive breeding programme would be for naught if there is not sufficient habitat to support the condors after release.' *Paul Ehrlich, ecologist*

In 1982 ten captive bred oryx were released into the wild in Oman. The Sultan has entrusted the Harasis, a small tribe of desert nomads, with the task of protecting them from poachers. It was poaching that led to their extinction in the wild. The bedouin hunted oryx on camel for centuries, but the introduction of the motorized shooting party by European civil servants and the Arabian aristocracy finally finished them off. If the oryx does survive in the wild – and there are plans to release more in Jordan – then it will

> 'Zoos' contribution to conservation will always be limited. At present it is frequently negative.' *Jon Bardzo and John Burton*

be the captive breeding programme which has saved it.

Zoos: a dismal record? Don't be fooled by the oryx project, many conservationists say. It is one of the very few captive breeding programmes that have been successful, so far. They may also concede that were it not for captive breeding, Père David's deer (from China), the European bison (from east Europe) and Przewalski's horse (from Mongolia) would probably all be extinct. Jon Bardzo and John Burton are two experts who have studied zoo breeding. They concluded that there are probably less than a dozen mammals with self-sustaining populations in zoos.

Zoos have three main functions: education, research and conservation. But are they the right place to conserve endangered species? Bardzo worked out that it is going to cost £22 million to keep the 800 Siberian tigers in captivity today until the end of the century. (There are probably only 400 Siberian tigers in the wild.) But what for, he asks. To reintroduce them into the wild? But will there be any wild habitat left by then? He concludes that the £22 million would be much better spent conserving the tiger's habitat, and thus the many other plants and animals with which it co-exists.

There are a few zoos whose sole purpose is to breed endangered species: a good example is Gerald Durrell's Jersey Wildlife Preservation Trust. But many appear guilty of doing wild populations more harm than good. However, does it matter if zoos fail to help conservation? Many consider them simply as high class circuses, there to entertain and educate.

Arabian oryx at the quarantine
station at Isiolo in northern
Kenya. Conservation in zoos
has saved the oryx from
extinction.

The danger list

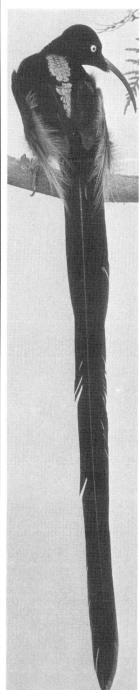

There are just 20 Seychelles magpie robins left; about 150 St Lucia parrots; 300 monkey-eating eagles; perhaps 50 Javan rhinoceroses; and less than 500 Simien foxes. All face imminent extinction.

There are between 5 and 10 million species of plant and animal in the world today. About 1.6 million have been identified. At the moment there is about one extinction a day, caused directly or indirectly by human activity. Experts like Norman Myers predict that a quarter of all species will be lost by the end of the century, which means there would be an average of 100 extinctions a day.

The threats, as this book has shown, are many and various. Some species are threatened by war: among them are scimitar horned oryx and addax in war-torn Chad, the Caspian tiger in Iran and Topi antelope in Uganda. Others are suffering at the hands of hunters and poachers. Among them may be counted many of the spotted and striped cats, elephants, rhinoceroses, crocodiles and a multitude of exotic birds and other animals unfortunate enough to have what man covets.

Most damaging of all, however, is loss of habitat. The destruction of tropical forests – which contain nearly half of all species – would be the greatest conceivable disaster for the natural world. However, widescale habitat destruction is not just confined to developing countries in the tropical zone. Since the last war Britain has lost more of her ancient broadleaved woodland – the richest of temperate habitats – than was destroyed during the preceding four centuries. Similarly, throughout the developed world, other

habitats have diminished in the face of agricultural and forestry pressures.

Disappearing species: anybody's guess?
It is easy to ridicule estimates of species extinction and Myers' figures may well reflect the pessimist's view. Other conservationists concede as much. However, this in no way lessens the gravity of the situation. A series of 'Red Data Books' have been compiled listing endangered species. They are very large books. There are already over 500 species – many mentioned here – which are so rare that all commercial trade in them and their derivatives has been prohibited.

The list is bound to get longer. Over half the known animal extinctions of the last two millennia have occurred since 1900. Is anything going to stop species extinctions increasing exponentially? The World Conservation Strategy, discussed overleaf, is one attempt to keep animals and plants off the danger list.

Far left New Guinea's birds of paradise have long been treasured for their bizarre and colourful plumage. Now they too are on the danger list.

Left The natterjack toad is now one of Britain's rarest creatures. Human disturbance and the destruction of its sand-dune breeding habitat have led to its dramatic decline this century.

Right Conservation projects may save the mountain gorilla in central Africa – or is that just wistful thinking?

The World Strategy

A few years ago the International Union for the Conservation of Nature (IUCN) managed to convince some other exceptionally powerful international organizations that the ecological deterioration of the planet had gone too far. In cooperation with the United Nations Environment Programme and the World Wildlife Fund, and with help from the UN's Food and Agriculture Organization, IUCN drew up a World Conservation Strategy (WCS). It was announced to the world in 1980.

> 'It is essential that the affluent constrain their demands on resources.' *World Conservation Strategy*

Many of the problems identified by the World Conservation Strategy have been touched on in this book: millions are compelled by poverty to destroy the resources on which they depend; resources required by industry are shrinking; the energy and financial costs of providing goods and services are ever increasing. The answer put forward by the WCS is that we must maintain ecological processes (which means, for example, looking after the soil); we must conserve a whole range of genetic diversity (which means conserving as great a range of species and genotypes as possible); and we must ensure that species and ecosystems are exploited in a sustainable manner.

Reception has been mixed. Many governments have applauded the intentions of the WCS but shown little enthusiasm for its advice. Many good ideas look like floundering amid the great international bureaucracies which have a habit of proliferating when everyone agrees that something needs to be done but no-one knows how. Others say bluntly that the WCS is a waste of time.

Despite government apathy, individual conservation bodies have done their best to produce national programmes of action in response to the WCS. However, the main fruits of the various committees which have been established to co-ordinate the programme have been mountains of paperwork. Although the WCS makes it clear that it is aimed as much at teachers, trade unionists, industrialists and resource managers as at politicians, there would seem little hope of it 'saving the world' if governments don't both accept its thesis and act on it.

Who will save the world? The WCS adopts a utilitarian approach to conservation: man's survival depends upon it. Development and conservation must go hand in hand.

In many ways, this is an uncontentious proposition. The head of the World Bank knows that there is no point putting money into agricultural developments which are unsustainable. The African peasant knows that he should not be felling wood for fuel faster than the trees can grow. And Atlantic fishermen know that the survival of their industry depends on the fish being harvested sensibly. These men may not talk of maximum sustainable yields – but they know exactly what they are.

But the crucial question still remains: how are man's activities to be controlled to the advantage of all and the detriment of none? Or, put another way: who will implement the World Conservation Strategy? However enlightened it is, many would claim that this is one question to which the WCS has found no answer.

Opposite These trees are their future. Indonesian students help on a re-afforestation project in the Dumoga National Park.

Conservation

'Converting the World Conservation Strategy into terms of street corner politics requires a work of genius.' Chris Rose, ecologist

A problem of

'If a free society cannot help the many who are poor, it cannot save the few who are rich.'
J. F. Kennedy, US president

poverty?

Refugees from the famine in northern Ethiopia. These villagers have left their parched lands in search of food. While wealth and natural resources are so unevenly shared and populations continue to soar, the future for increasing numbers in the world's poor countries is as bleak as this Ethiopian landscape.

> **'The poor and illiterate are usually and conveniently silent.'** *J. K. Galbraith, economist*

In the early 1970s (according to Global 2000, the study commissioned by US President Jimmy Carter) one hectare of arable land supported 2.6 persons. By the year 2000 that hectare will have to support 4 people. As most of the earth's good land is already cultivated, the increase in food must come from higher yields.

Yet to get higher yields even greater quantities of energy – in the form of fuel, fertilizers and so forth – will be required. Energy resources are becoming increasingly scarce and expensive. Thus, in the quest to increase world food supplies, more marginal lands – forests, swamps, savannahs – will inevitably be brought into some form of cultivation.

Feeding the world is the most pressing problem today. The United Nations estimates that there are 500 million malnourished and 800 million destitute in the world. The vast majority of these people live in rural areas. The World Conservation Strategy suggested that they are being forced to destroy the environment in which they find themselves. If this is true, then many of the problems discussed in this book are the result of poverty. Does this mean that conservation is more a question of distributive justice than of creating national parks and nature reserves?

A political issue? Twenty or even ten years ago conservation was largely the preoccupation of those nations who could afford it. It was considered a luxury. Many now believe it has become a necessity.

No longer does the word conservation simply evoke pictures of vast herds of game wandering across African plains. Desertification, overfishing, pollution: these are now the crucial questions of conservation. The fate of the cheetah or the hartebeest may not concern many; but the state of our croplands, our forests and our fisheries affects all of us. Thus over a very short period of time conservation has become a political issue.

According to the World Conservation Strategy, 'much habitat destruction and over-exploitation of living resources by individuals, communities and nations in the developing world is a response to relative poverty, caused or exacerbated by a combination of human population growth and inequities within and among nations'. Those who take this view see salvation coming from the rich shifting some of their wealth to the poor and at the same time reducing their own consumption of resources (one Swiss consumes the same as 40 Somalis).

There are many who may be unconvinced by the conservationists' arguments but who will endorse, on moral grounds, the plea that the earth's resources be shared more equitably. The future – both for a large chunk of humanity (by the year 2000 four out of five people will live in developing countries) and for the world's wildlife – is extremely uncertain. Much may depend on whether governments and world leaders (in both rich and poor countries) accept the environmentalists' critical prognosis; and even more importantly, on whether they bother to act on it.

Reference

Further reading

There is a voluminous literature dealing with most of the subjects touched on in this book. Unfortunately much of it is to be found in scattered articles in newspapers, journals and scientific periodicals. Although a few species get an entire book to themselves, most must be content with passing references. However, the books listed below provide an excellent introduction to world conservation.

Down to Earth by Erik Eckholm (Pluto Press, 1982) is one of the most perceptive works on the problems of integrating development with conservation. It deserves to stand alongside the classic *Only One Earth* by Barbara Ward and René Dubos (Penguin, 1972). Among the books which deal specifically with poverty (though not explicitly with its relationship to environmental degradation) are Susan George's *How the Other Half Dies* (Penguin, 1976) and John Cole's *The Poor of the Earth* (Macmillan, 1976). Both are fine books. The business of how the world must feed itself is capably dealt with by Lester Brown in *By Bread Alone* (Pergamon, 1975). Norman Myers presents a lively but gloomy analysis of the problem of endangered species in *The Sinking Ark* (Pergamon, 1979) and the enormous *Cousteau Almanac: An Inventory of Life on Our Water Planet* by Jacques-Yves Cousteau and his staff (Dolphin Books, 1981) tackles every conceivable aspect of conservation.

One of the best accounts of a specific conservation project in action is Guy Mountford's *Saving the Tiger* (Michael Joseph, 1981). The Animal Welfare Institute's *Facts About Furs* (3rd ed. 1980) and *The Bird Business* by Greta Nilssen (Animal Welfare Institute, 1981) are admirable guides to the slaughter and trade in animals and birds. There are three good books partly or wholly about pesticides and their effects on the natural world. *Silent Spring* by Rachel Carson (Hamish Hamilton, 1962) is justifiably famous and was highly influential in the decade which saw environmentalism become a popular movement. Kenneth Mellanby's *Pesticides and Pollution* (Collins, 1967) is still worth reading,

and David Bull's *A Growing Problem: Pesticides and the Third World Poor* (Oxfam, 1982) is a particularly fine book.

There are three further books, all by institutions rather than individuals, which deserve special attention. These are *The World Conservation Strategy* (IUCN, 1980), *North South: A Programme for Survival* by the Brandt Commission (Pan, 1980), and *Global 2000* by the US Interagency Committee (US Government Printing Office, 1980). The first of these has been popularized by Robert Allen in *How to Save the World* (Kogan Page, 1980).

Turning to Britain, Richard Mabey's *The Common Ground* (Hutchinson, 1980) is an eloquent plea for conservation and *Paradise Lost* (Friends of the Earth, 1981) by Czech Conroy and Angela King gives the facts which show we need it. Marion Shoard provides a strong attack on the rural ravages of the farming industry in *The Theft of the Countryside* (Temple Smith, 1980) and *Crisis and Conservation* (Penguin, 1984) by Charlie Pye-Smith and Chris Rose gives an analysis of both the industries which threaten wildlife and the organizations which are trying to save the countryside. Max Nicholson is one of the grand old men of conservation—both in Britain and elsewhere—and his book *The Environmental Revolution: A Guide to the New Masters of the World* (Pelican, 1972) remains both provocative and stimulating. For the serious student of the conservation movement, Timothy O'Riordan's *Environmentalism* (Pion, 1981) is indispensable. Finally, there is one book which says little about species conservation but which should be read by all those who doubt whether man and nature can co-exist: E.F. Schumacher's *Small is Beautiful: A Study of Economics as if People Mattered* (Blond and Briggs, 1973) may convince them otherwise.

Who's who in conservation

The most prominent conservation body acting globally is the **International Union for the Conservation of Nature and Natural Resources** (IUCN). Founded in 1948, IUCN has almost 500 member organizations in 111 countries. IUCN provides much of the expertise for conservation work carried out with the financial backing of the **World Wildlife Fund** (WWF). Details of all WWF projects are given in the organization's Yearbook. WWF International is based at 1196 Gland, Switzerland. However, many countries have their own branches of the WWF. The British one was founded in 1961 (Panda House, 12-13 Ockford Road, Godalming, Surrey). Nearly every country in the world has a government organization charged with conserving nature, though many are minor parts of departments whose main work involves the promotion of activities often inimical to good conservation. These organizations – in Britain they are the **Nature Conservancy Council** (19/20 Belgrave Square, London SW1) and the **Countryside Commission** (John Dower House, Crecent Place, Cheltenham, Glos.) – are funded by governments and though their activities can be of great importance they are often unable to campaign vigorously on key issues. The NCC manages nearly 200 nature reserves covering more than 135,000 hectares. The Commission helps to run the country's national parks.

Those who wish to become seriously involved in environmental work must turn to the voluntary (non-governmental) organizations in their country. The most prominent campaigning conservation groups in Britain are **Greenpeace** (whose International Council is at Temple House, 25/26 High Street, Lewes, Sussex) and **Friends of the Earth** (377 City Road, London EC1). Both organizations have international networks and supply their members with information and literature about their campaigns. Considering its meagre resources, Greenpeace has been spectacularly successful in drawing public attention to the fate of the whales, to seal hunting in Canada and to the dumping of toxic and nuclear wastes at sea. FoE campaigns vigorously on subjects as varied as bicycles to acid rain and habitat conservation.

Among the most powerful conservation bodies in Britain are the **National Trust** (42 Queen Anne's Gate, London SW1) and the **Royal Society for the Protection of Birds** (The Lodge, Sandy, Bedfordshire). Both have large numbers of members (the Trust over a million) and own much property. Though the Trust's main interests revolve round stately homes, it has much land of conservation value. The RSPB manages some of the greatest bird reserves in the country.

For those who wish to get their hands dirty the county naturalists' trusts (all of which come under the administrative umbrella of the **Royal Society for Nature Conservation**, The Green, Nettleham, Lincoln) and the **British Trust for Conservation Volunteers** (10-14 Duke Street, Reading, Berkshire) are worth contacting. They will be pleased to get your money if not your help.

Finally, there are many rather more scholastic organizations prominent in the conservation world. One which manages to combine practical conservation with academic investigation is the **Fauna and Flora Preservation Society** (c/o Zoological Society of London, Regent's Park, London NW1). The Oryx Project is one of many international schemes supported by ffPS.

Laws and conventions

Most countries have afforded some legal protection to wildlife. Those with the most comprehensive systems of protection tend to be the industrialized nations of the western world. However, this doesn't necessarily mean they are the most conservation-minded. Indeed countries like Britain only acted long after most of their natural habitat had been cleared, and many conservationists believe that the Wildlife and Countryside Act is woefully inadequate. During the 1960s and early 1970s the United States could justifiably consider itself one of the world's most enlightened countries in the field of conservation. But times have changed. President Reagan, unlike some of his predecessors, has no time for conservation and some of America's best wildlife legislation has been scrapped.

There are now four key international conservation treaties. One of the most important is CITES, the **Convention on International Trade in Endangered Species of Wild Fauna and Flora.** CITES had undoubtedly helped to stem the trade, and thus the slaughter, of many wild creatures. However, although over 80 countries have ratified the convention, there remain even more who have not, and smuggling of many wildlife products still continues. In many instances customs officers don't have the necessary training and knowledge to be able to distinguish between those creatures which are protected under CITES and those which aren't. European conservationists are concerned about the Common Market becoming a single member of CITES. Trade between the ten countries will not be monitored and CITES will only be as strong as its weakest link. Belgium has a poor record as a wildlife trader, and it is not certain that it will fall into line.

The **Ramsar Convention on Wetlands of International Importance, Especially as Waterfowl Habitat** was drawn up in 1971. As its long-winded name implies, its purpose is to protect wetlands from pollution, agricultural reclamation and industrial damage. Although Britain's Nature Conservancy Council identified over a hundred sites worthy of designation (Britain is particularly important for wildfowl and wading birds) the Department of the Environment, which is the NCC's paymaster, has formally listed only 19 of these.

Most conservationists had heard little about the **World Heritage Convention** before the fuss blew up over the proposed Franklin Dam in Tasmania. Over eighty countries have ratified the Convention and its purpose is to protect the world's greatest sites of cultural and natural importance: thus the Pyramids qualify alongside the Tasmanian Wilderness. The IUCN has produced a draft list which it hopes countries will adopt for designation as World Heritage Sites. The two recommended for Britain are the Cairngorms Massif in central Scotland and St Kilda, the magnificent bird island flung far out in the Atlantic. Recognition as a Heritage Site undoubtedly helped save the Tasmanian Wilderness so the Convention may not be the paper tiger which many had suspected.

Finally there is the **Bonn Convention on the Conservation of Migratory Species of Wild Animals.** This is a potentially most important treaty though only 15 countries have so far ratified it. On the positive side, this includes Italy, a country with a disgraceful record of slaughtering birds on their annual migrations; on the negative side, few of the countries are contiguous (an intriguing exception is Israel and Egypt). Unfortunately animals and plants recognize no national boundaries. Warblers which receive vigilant protection in northern Europe are quite likely to find themselves diverted from their journey to Africa via a pickle jar in Naples or Barcelona. Similarly the great herds of herbivores that wander across the African savannahs get a better reception in some countries than in others. It is thus of vital importance to many species that this convention is made to work. Countries which have ratified it are: Denmark, Hungary, Ireland, Italy, Luxembourg, the Netherlands, Portugal and Sweden in Europe; Egypt and Israel in the Middle East; Cameroon and Niger in Africa; Chile in South America; and India in the Far East.

Index

Numbers in **bold** refer to illustration captions

Credits

Aldus Archive: 9
Bryan and Cherry Alexander
Photography: 29 (right)
Ardea: cover
McDougal/Ardea: 19
Valerie Taylor/Ardea: 21
David and Kate Urry/Ardea: 44
(top)
Barnaby's Picture Library: 11
(top), 25
Camera Press: 23, 27, 35
J. Allen Cash: 22, 42, 44
(bottom), 53
Earthscan: 5, 16, 30, 37
Mark Edwards/Earthscan: 6, 8,
17
Marcos Santilli/Earthscan: 13
Greenpeace: 28
Eric Hosking: 32, 38-9, 48, 54
(right), 55
Niall Rankin/Eric Hosking: 47,
50-51
Howard Payton/Rare Breeds
Survival Trust: 11 (bottom)
Piers Cavendish/Save the
Children: 14
Mike Wells/Save the Children: 58
Tony Morrison/South American
Pictures: 24
P. Scharma/World Health
Organization: 40
Kenya Information
Service/World Wildlife Fund:
33
W. S. Peckover/World Wildlife
Fund: 54 (left)
Berend Wegman/World Wildlife
Fund: 57

Picture research by Diana
Morris; design by Paul May